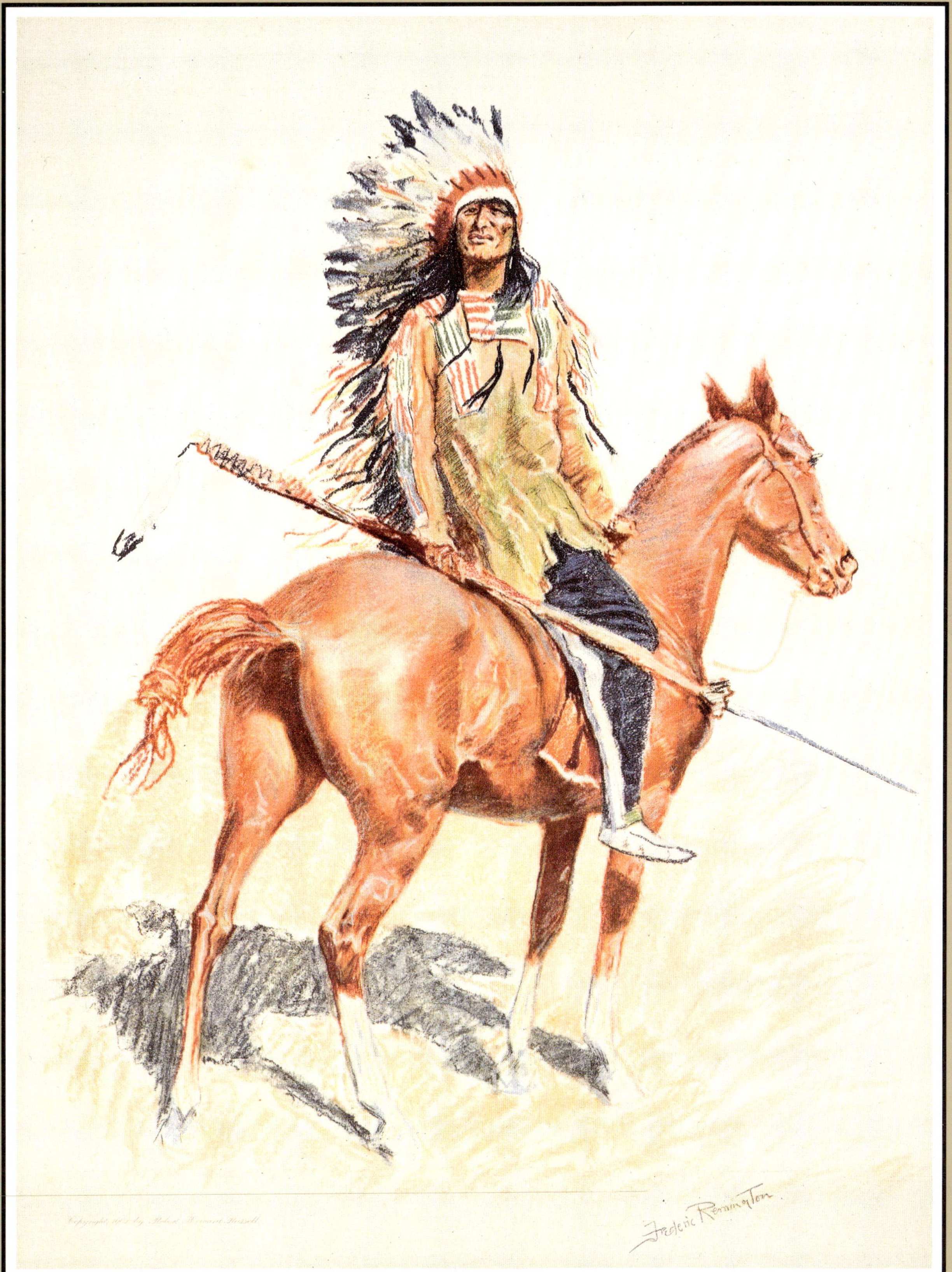
Frederic Remington

A Sioux Chief. By Frederic Remington. From *A Bunch of Buckskins,* 1901.

Published by Dover Publications, Inc.
31 East 2nd Street
Mineola, N.Y. 11501.

A Cavalry Officer. By Frederic Remington. From *A Bunch of Buckskins,* 1901.

Published by Dover Publications, Inc.
31 East 2nd Street
Mineola, N.Y. 11501.

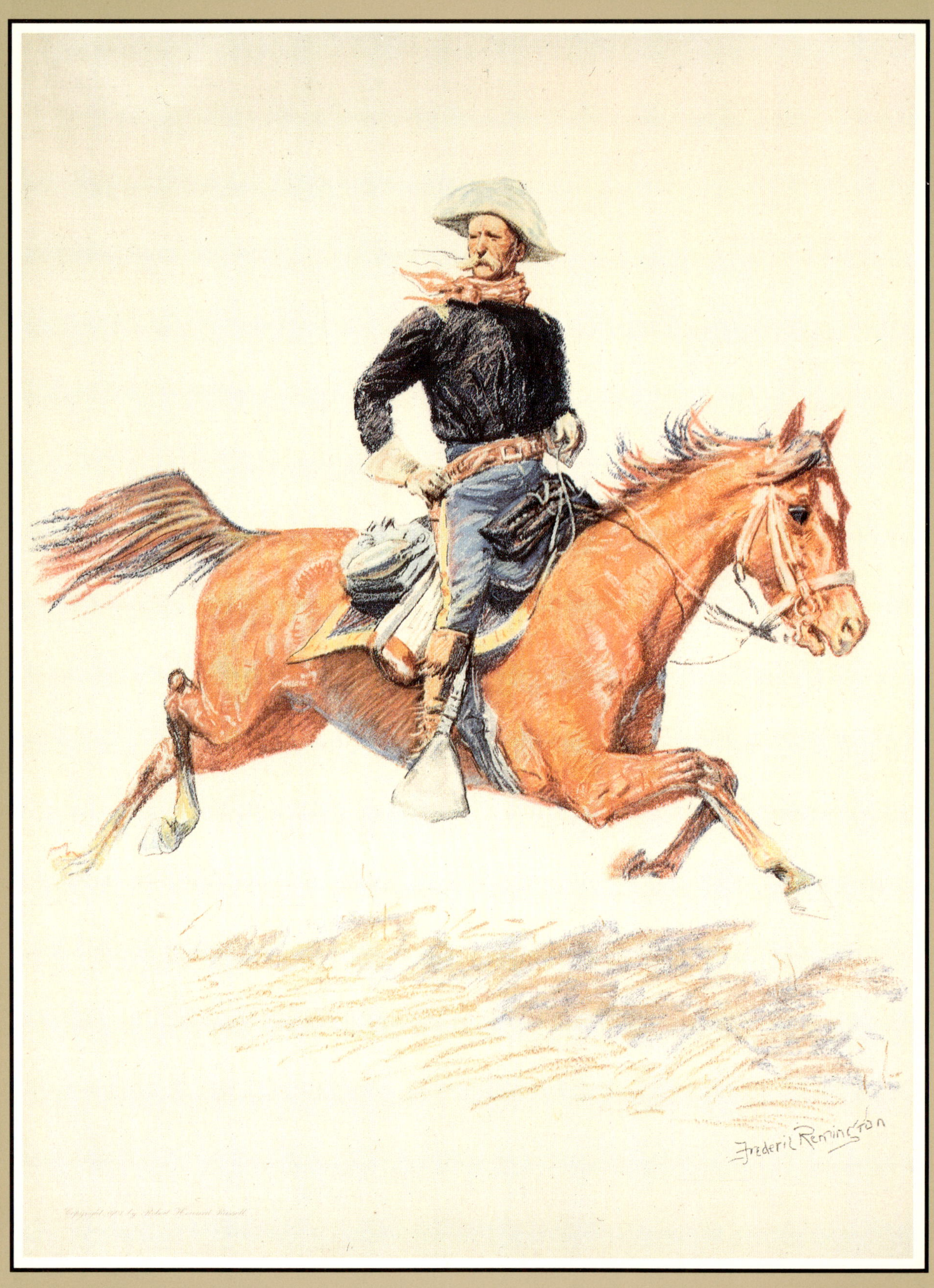

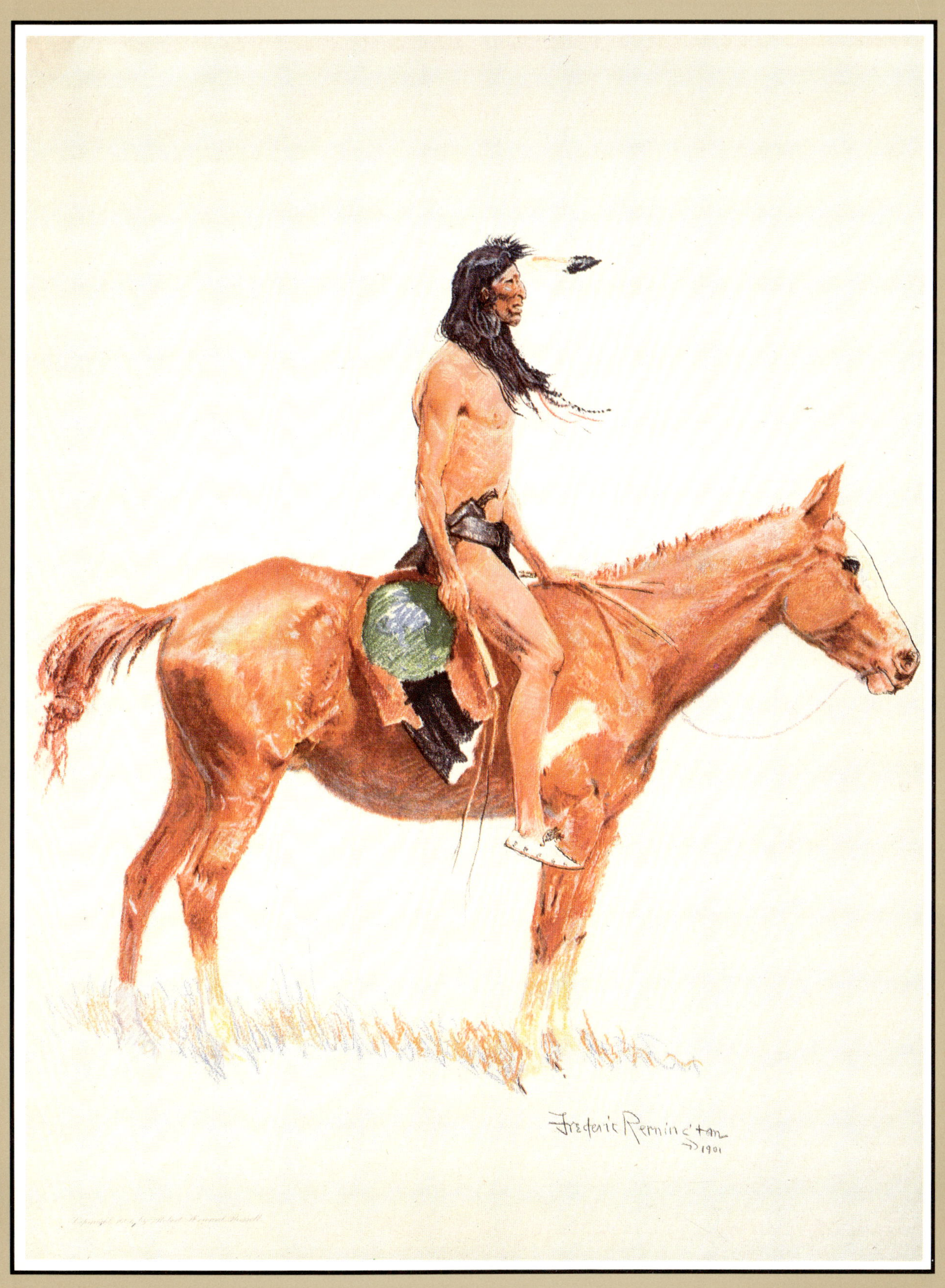

A Cheyenne Buck. By Frederic Remington. From *A Bunch of Buckskins,* 1901.

Published by Dover Publications, Inc.
31 East 2nd Street
Mineola, N.Y. 11501.

Old Ramon. By Frederic Remington. From *A Bunch of Buckskins,* 1901.

Published by Dover Publications, Inc.
31 East 2nd Street
Mineola, N.Y. 11501.

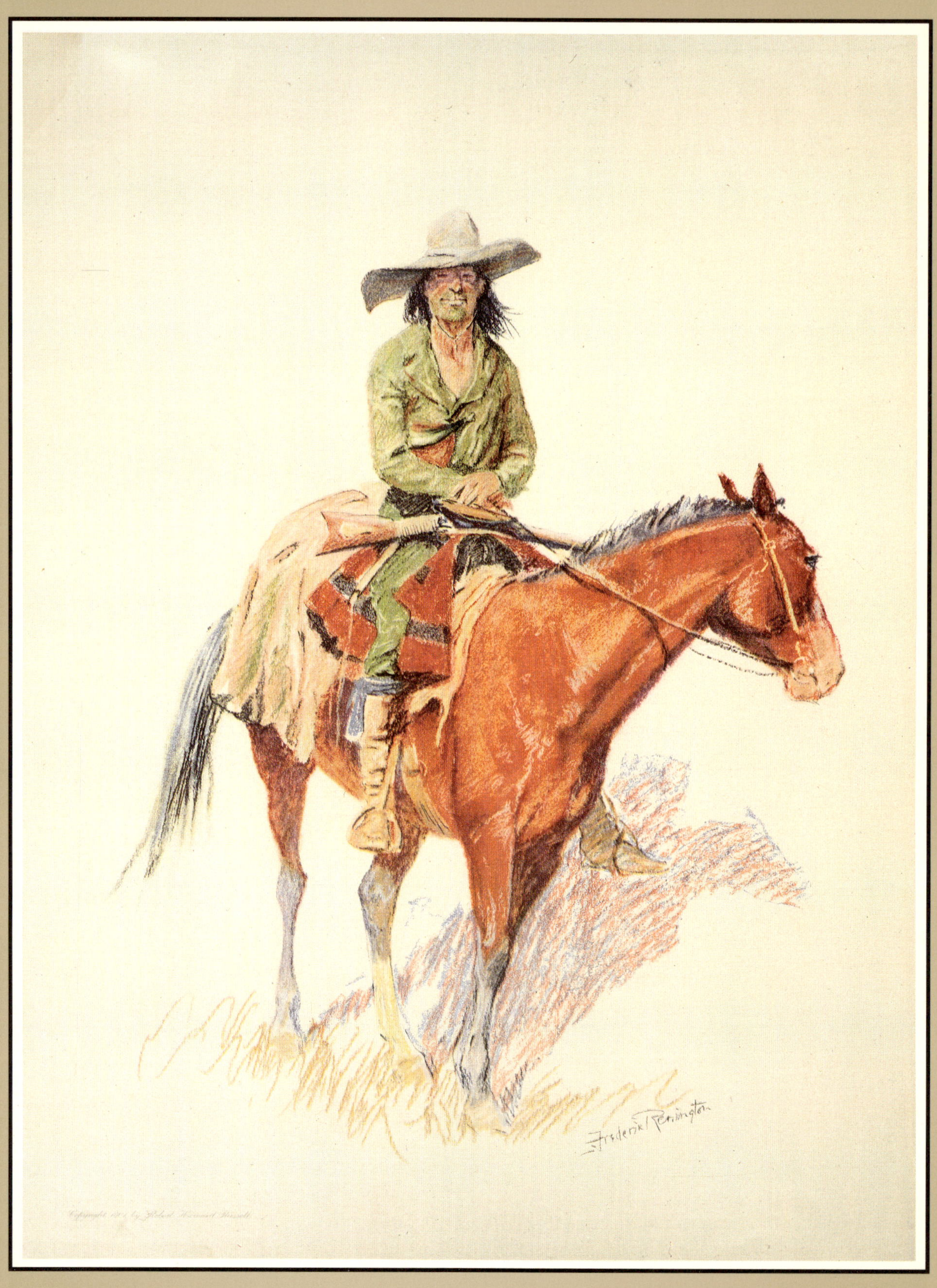
Frederic Remington

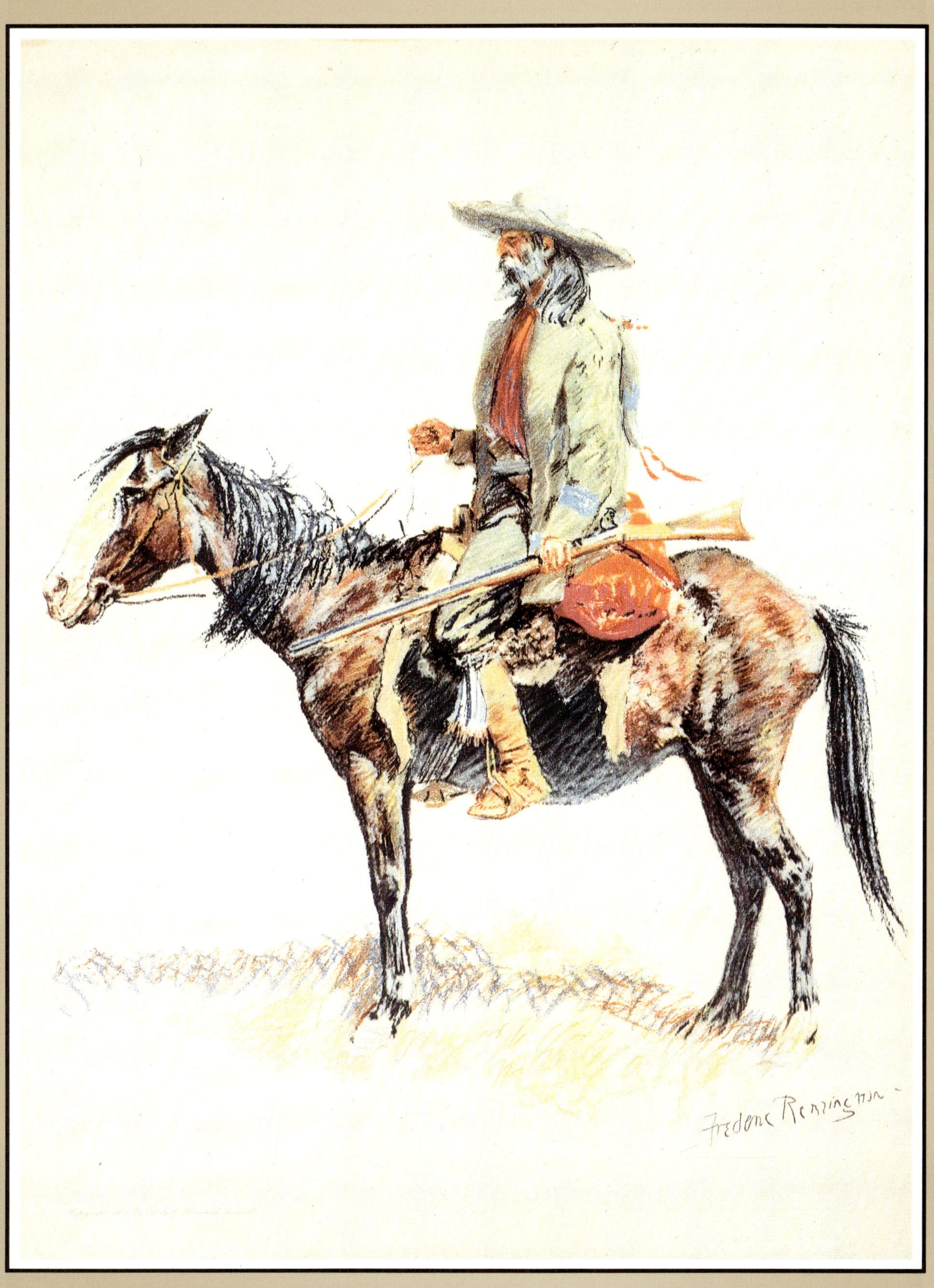
Frederic Remington

A Trapper. By Frederic Remington. From *A Bunch of Buckskins,* 1901.

Published by Dover Publications, Inc.
31 East 2nd Street
Mineola, N.Y. 11501.

A Breed. By Frederic Remington. From *A Bunch of Buckskins,* 1901.

Published by Dover Publications, Inc.
31 East 2nd Street
Mineola, N.Y. 11501.

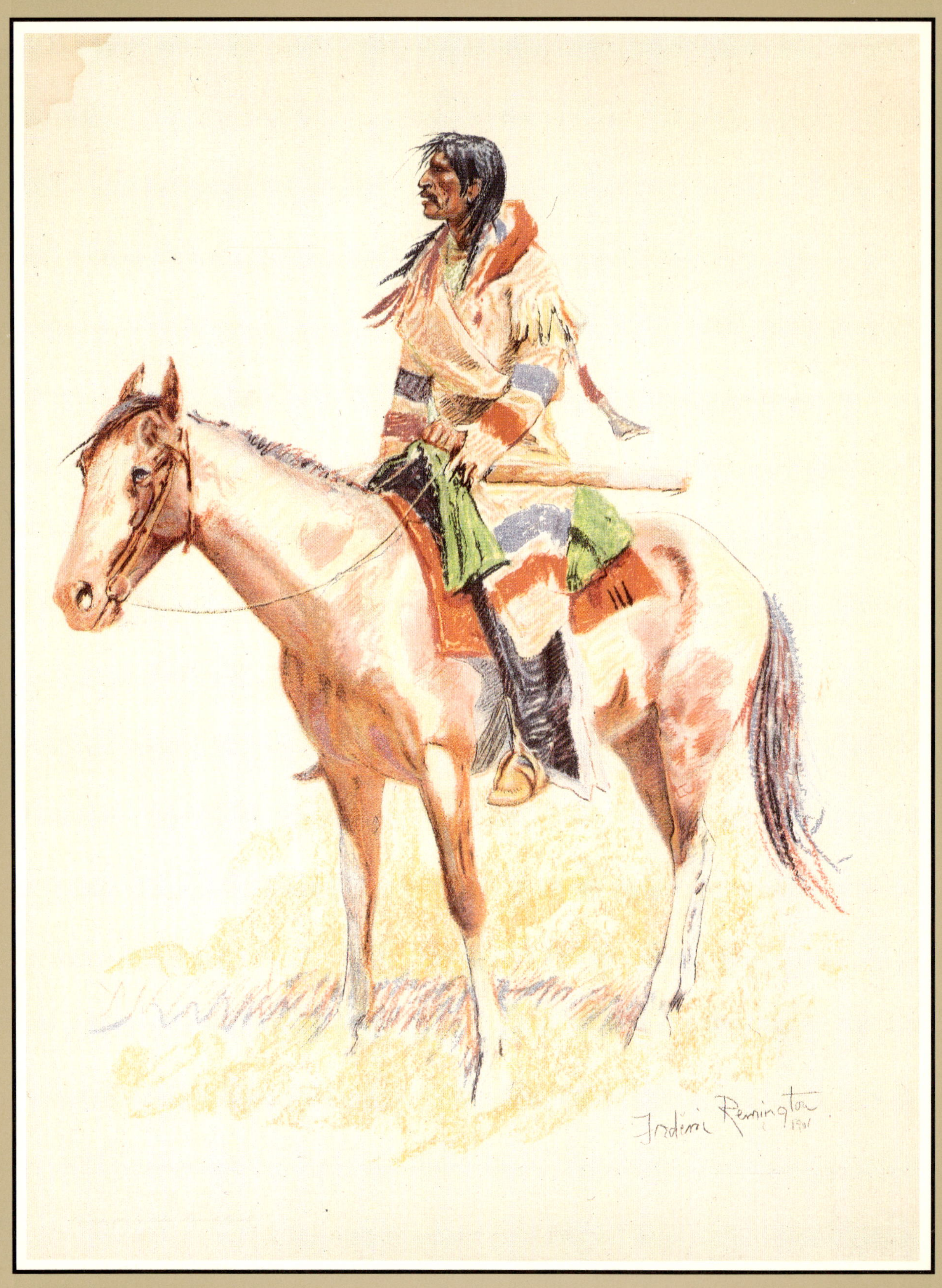

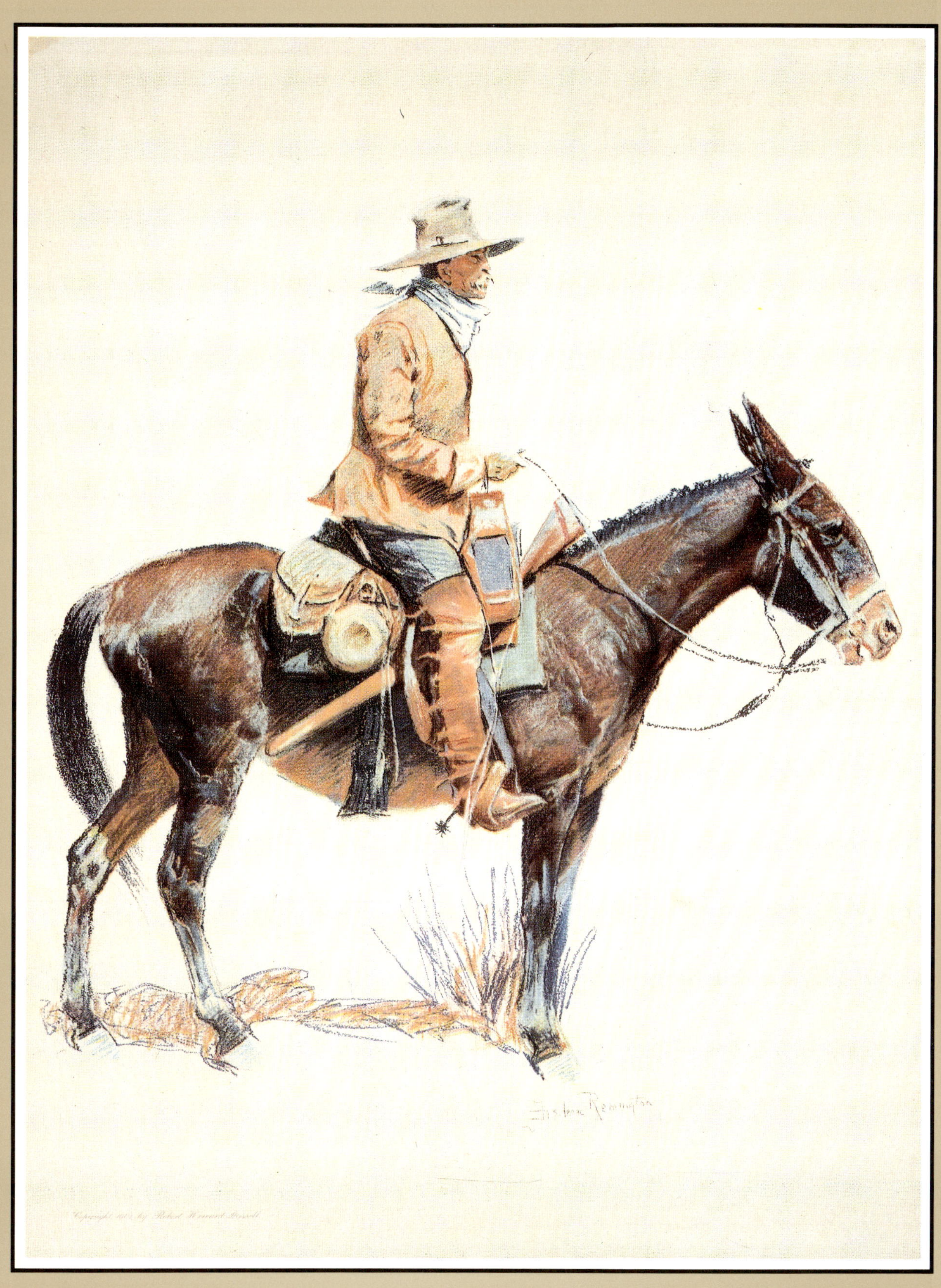

An Army Packer. By Frederic Remington. From *A Bunch of Buckskins*, 1901.

Published by Dover Publications, Inc.
31 East 2nd Street
Mineola, N.Y. 11501.

An Arizona Cowboy. By Frederic Remington. From *A Bunch of Buckskins,* 1901.

Published by Dover Publications, Inc.
31 East 2nd Street
Mineola, N.Y. 11501.

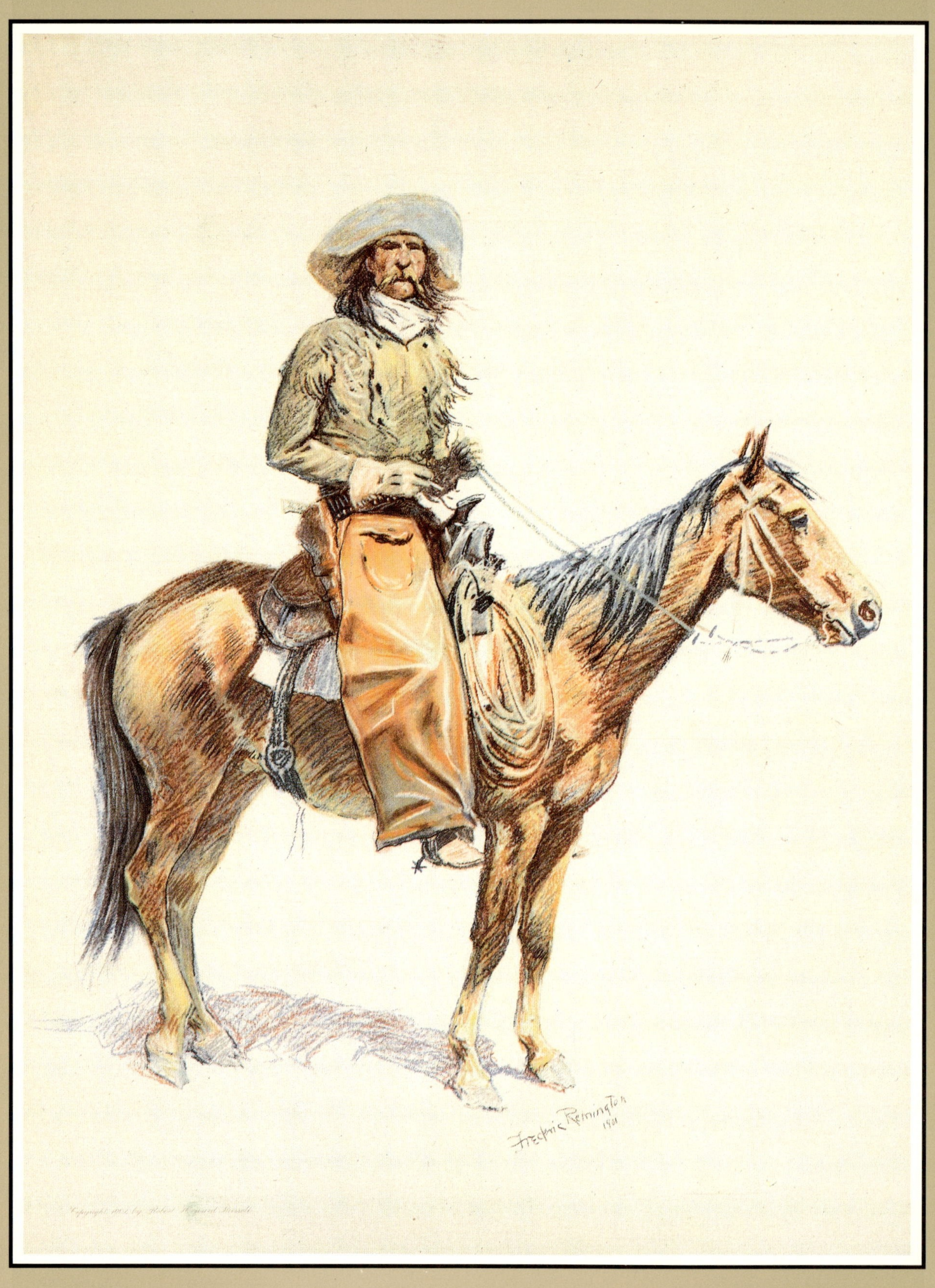
Frederic Remington
1901